PALATI NATUS Rheni

Mil. Germanica 1 2 3 50

Historic map labels: Weykirchen, Selingstat, Dieborg, Oftheim, Sulßbag, Eisenbach, Swungenberg, Wirt, Laudenbach, Miltenburg, Prenberg, Lindenh, Furstenw, Michelst, Weynheim, schriessen, Hirßhorn, Leymen, Ketfch, Wiseloch, Byfch, Sintzen, Eppingen, Ochsenzei, Kinding, Maulbronn, Staim, Kirchb, Homburg, Karlsberg, Vaihing, Enntz

Modern map labels: Langenlonsheim, Bad Kreuznach, nach Mainz, Bad Münster, Ebernburg, Altenbaumburg, Nahe, Odernheim, Obermoschel, Alsenz, nach Mainz, Meisenheim, Kirchheimbolanden, nach Idar-Oberstein, Lauterecken, Offenbach, Donnersberg, Bockenheim, Burg Lichtenberg, Grünstadt, Laumersheim, nach St. Wendel, Kusel, Neu-Leiningen, Frankenthal, Otterberg, Herxheim a. B., Enkenbach, Alt-Leiningen, Kallstadt, Ludwigshafen, Ungstein, Hardenburg, Bad Dürkheim, Kaiserslautern, Wachenheim, Landstuhl, Hohenecken, Forst, Deidesheim, Königsbach, Ruppertsberg, Karls tal, Trippstadt, Elmstein, Lambrecht, Gimmeldingen, Schifferstadt, Johannis Kreuz, Mußbach, Karlsberg, Neustadt, Homburg, Heldenstein, Hambach, Speyer, St. Martin, Diedesfeld, Zweibrücken, Taubenstuhl, Maikammer, Merzalben, Weyher, Edenkoben, Rhodt, Burrweiler, Germersheim, nach Bruchsal, Hornbach, Albersweiler, Bellheim, Annweiler, Pirmasens, Hint.-Weidenthal, Leinsweiler, Landau, Dahn, Lindelbrunn, Klingenmünster, Drachenfels, nach Karlsruhe, Dörrenbach, Bergzabern, Schweigen

In the Heart of the Palatinate

A LEISURELY JOURNEY
FROM KREUZNACH TO SPEYER

PICTURES RUDOLF SCHULER

TEXT DR. RICHARD HENK

DRAWINGS HEINZ MICHEL

VERLAG BRAUSDRUCK GMBH HEIDELBERG

Translated by Charlotte Fuhrmann

Second revised edition

Frankish emperors and their officials, the counts on the Rhine, gave the Palatinate its name and its first geographical boundaries. The early Frankish-Lorraine counts originally had their seat in Aachen, on the Lower Rhine or on the Moselle. But Hermann von Stahleck's ancestral castle was above Bacharach and Konrad von Staufen already ruled the country not far from Alzey. The Salian rulers first chose Worms as their burial place, until, after becoming emperors, they changed it to Speyer.

In the early days large stretches of the country were also administered by monasteries. The most important of these were the monasteries of Weissenburg, Lorsch, Hornbach and the cathedral chapter of Worms. The cultivation of the land was soon furthered especially by the rapidly growing Cistercian order. Their great monastery church at Otterberg, of majestic proportions, still looms above the little town of Otterbach.

But the real existence of the Palatinate may be said to date from the time when the title of Count Palatine was bestowed on the Wittelsbachs. In spite of many troubled times, this Bavarian line was able with only a few breaks to rule the country till 1918. As Electors, the Counts Palatine were soon among the seven most powerful princes of the Holy Roman Empire. Their power was rounded off and the right to the office of Lord High Steward (Erztruchsess) was given them by the Golden Bull of 1356.

A long series of names designate the rulers who had their residence at the castle in Heidelberg. Thus Ruprecht I founded Heidelberg University, which took the place of Prague as the oldest German university after the break-up of the old empire. But the Wittelsbach kings did not always have luck on their side. Even under King Ruprecht conditions in the weakened empire were unfavorable for him and his government.

The most popular Count Elector is probably Friedrich the Victorious. But the victories of "Pfälzer Fritz", as he was called, were not achieved without fighting and the villages of the Vorderpfalz, in and bordering on the Rhine plain, were the sufferers. People of Landau and Bergzabern spoke of him only as the "Wicked Fritz". In the battle near Seckenheim in 1462 he finally defeated his last antagonists. The Margrave of Baden and the Count of Württemberg were led through Heidelberg as prisoners and confined in the keep of the castle.

New devastation was brought upon the land by the War of the Palatine-Bavarian Succession. The destruction at this time was only surpassed by that suffered later on under the French. Even the proud monastery of Limburg, Emporer Konrad's favorite place of worship, was destroyed by fire.

From this time on the Count Electors avoided military entanglements. Thus the peasants were able to burn Altleiningen Castle without hindrance. It was not until their troops had dared to cross the Rhine that they met with total defeat at Pfeddersheim. Franz von Sickingen was long allowed to carry on his various feuds undisturbed. When the knight finally turned against the Count Elector of Trier, Palatine troops came to the aid of the hard-pressed Trier forces.

During the first years of the Reformation the Count Electors Palatine were undecided. Otthein-rich was the first to introduce the Lutheran confession. He is the same ruler who added to Heidelberg Castle a strikingly beautiful building in early Renaissance style. From the period of his successor, Friedrich III, dates the Heidelberg Catechism, one of the most important documents of the reformed church. After the revocation of the Edict of Nantes Huguenots poured into the country in large numbers and founded the cities of Lambrecht and Frankenthal, which, thanks to their skill as clothmakers, became new centers of trade.

The succession passed eventually to a Catholic branch of the Wittelsbachs. Many churches were divided by walls in order to make room for the various confessions. Even today a wall separates nave and transept of the old monastery church of Otterberg, making it impossible for the visitor to get a full impression of the majestic vaulting of the former Cistercian abbey.

The Elisabeth Gate and the English Building call to mind the last king of the Heidelberg line. Friedrich V. owes his title, however, to the revolt of the Bohemian Diet. Soon after, in the battle of the Weissen Berg, the "Winter King" lost his throne and all his other prerogatives. The famous Heidelberg collection of manuscripts found its way to the papal library. Worse still was the loss of Landau and Philippsburg, which served the French army as important bases for attack.

The Palatinate was able to enjoy only a brief breathing space after the Thirty Years War. In 1677 the armies of Louis XIV destroyed most of the villages in the Wasgau. The marriage of "Liselotte of the Palatinate" with the Duke of Orleans was used by the roi soleil as a pretext for further claims and invasions. No other part of the old empire had to endure such complete devastation. Heidelberg and Mannheim on the right bank of the Rhine suffered the same fate of scorched earth (Louis XIV is said to have given the command "Brulez le Palatinat!"). When the armies of the roi soleil were finally forced to withdraw, they left behind them only smouldering ruins. The monuments of artistic value in the country, in so far as they survived at all, still bear the mark of those years and are most of them mutilated.

The Palatinate was not able to recover completely from this disaster. The country passed by inheritance to the Bavarian branch of the Wittelsbachs and Karl Philipp used a quarrel with the Heidelberg authorities as a pretext to move his residence to Mannheim. There he erected one of the largest Baroque castles in Germany.

Otterberg Monastery

The Rococo period in the Palatinate is connected with the name of Count Elector Karl Theodor, who had a passion for building. One of the most notable structures of this time is the Old Bridge in Heidelberg, much praised by poets and a masterpiece of late Baroque architecture. Karl Theodor's residence, Mannheim, was a cultural center visited by such figures as Voltaire, Lessing and the young Schiller. Mozart found here a large orchestra, by the standards of the period, still playing in the spirit of Stamitz. Karl Theodor showed an active interest in economic questions. Frankenthal received his support for its textile factories and for locks to connect the new industry with the Rhine. The years of his long rule are the last high spot in the history of the Palatinate and at the same time bring the period to a close. In 1777 the Count Elector, on inheriting Bavaria, had to move his residence to Munich.

The Palatinate, which had been one of the pillars of the old empire, was thus reduced to the status of a remote Bavarian province.

The People of the Palatinate

There is nothing in the nature of the people of the Palatinate to show the hard trials to which history has subjected them. They are always on top of the world, enjoying the fun of the moment and ready to overwhelm their guests with a volley of jokes. Where merriment is, there they are always to be found, though under the surface the picture may be a different one.

Some may think that the people of the Palatinate are easy to understand. They are always ready for a chat and after a while the questioner thinks he knows his man through and through. But far from it! The people of the Palatinate make friends with everyone easily and their cordiality includes everyone they like. A real friendship, however, requires more than that. But if they are convinced of the sincere response of the other, they are not likely to ask how long they have been acquainted. If another shows undue curiosity or even tries to play a trick on him, the man from the Palatinate finds it easy to evade him, with the humorous twinkle of the person who knows his own worth. To judge the people of the Palatinate merely by what they say, is to touch only the surface. True, they sometimes laugh more at their own jokes than their audience does, they can be a bit too loud and earn their nickname of "Pfälzer Krischer" (literally "Palatine shouter"). But no guest can compete with them in fluency of speech! Their nimble wits have often puzzled the members of the French occupation. The latter have never been quite sure how they stand with them. The people of the Palatinate are unsurpassed as masters of the ancient game of fooling the rest of the world. They are "smart guys", who know very well what they want. How else could they ever have survived the turmoils of Palatine history!

The inhabitants of the Palatinate have a sixth sense for everything happening around them. Long before others are disturbed, they have sensed the danger; their imagination has already conjured up a picture before their neighbors have even begun to think about it. If they go on cheerfully, showing nothing outwardly, it is because they have learned that being afraid doesn't help matters.

As good observers, they understand how to get along with people. Over a glass of wine, they are aware not only of the qualities of the wine itself but of the subtle change the Riesling produces in the face of the other, as warmth, good cheer and relaxation show their effect. They observe quietly, leaving the atmosphere undisturbed.

When a discussion has reached a deadlock, they have the gift of relieving tension by a joke at the right moment. Much as they enjoy disputation and fencing with words, they never bear a grudge. On the contrary, they are by nature conciliatory.

They are always a bit ahead of the others. While the Swabians are still considering a matter, the Saxons have half solved it and the people of the Rhineland have begun talking about it, the people of the Palatinate have long since taken action. They are quick to form an opinion and equally quick to draw conclusions from it.

The people of the Palatinate know how to enjoy life! They savor their hours of pleasure as they do their Spätlese, to the last drop. They steal time for it without seeming to do so. Relaxation and enjoyment are to them one and the same. They feel nothing but pity for those who have little that is pleasant or delightful, little that is sunny to look back on. And yet at the same time the people of the Palatinate are hard-working and industrious, and more than once they have transformed their land from a wilderness into a blossoming garden. Their imagination concerns itself with their everyday life and the smallest detail is of importance and worth describing. It is not an accident that the visitor everywhere comes upon humorous plays written in dialect.

The people of the Palatinate create their picture of the world from what they see about them. It must have brilliant colors, the glowing red of the sandstone soil, the deep reddish blue of the Portugieser grapes and the greenish blue with a touch of black of the pine woods. The painter Slevogt in Neukastell used on his canvases colors such as would meet with their approval. The dry, burnt smell of the Palatine forest in summer, the steaming Rhine plain emerging in new freshness from a thunder shower, these must have a place in the picture, as well as the fragrance of roses and lilies in the front gardens.

Even when clouds cover the sky and there is no more blue to be seen, in a world grown grave and dark, the people of the Palatinate remain half thoughtful jesters, half smiling philosophers. They have not forgotten how to laugh, to joke and to enjoy a good hearty meal. But they are very well aware how little the efforts of the individual avail against the powers of this world.

Towards the Palatinate

Klopp Castle and the long Rüdesheim hillside mark the place where the Nahe and the Rhine meet. The Drusus Bridge, resting on old Roman foundations, connects the steep banks of the Nahe, where some of Bingen's best-known vineyards are located. A flat, fertile landscape borders the road southwards. Those interested in wine should stop for a mid-morning glass at *Langenlonsheim* or *Münster-Sarmsheim*. The taste still hints that the Rhine is not far away. There is not only bouquet but also a prickling, sparkling character in the Riesling or Sylvaner that shows it is half related to the Moselle wines. But only half related! In youthful freshness and sunny early ripeness, which seems to anticipate the later development of the wine, the vineyards along the Nahe can compete with any other wine-growing area. But to experience the full roundness of Nahe wine, the visitor must wait till *Bad Kreuznach*.

The Nahe is a friendly river as it winds its way through the famous watering place, leaving plenty of room for row-boats and kayaks in its inlets. Guests taking the cure there may find distraction from their cares in the gentle lapping of the river along the banks of the Rose Island. In the valley of the saline the graduation works stretch out like mediaeval bastions in the meadows. The brine must drip down seven times through the blackthorn twigs of the works, formerly property of the Counts Palatine, before it can be made into salt in the pans of the salt refinery, or into the valuable mother liquor which is added to the baths.

The visitor can wander through the Old Town for hours constantly coming upon new vistas. The little streams that went by the old houses of the tanners are now underground. Under the foundations of the beautiful Church of St. Nicholas there still flows a broad current that makes the church pleasantly cool on hot summer days. In the Egg Market and the Salt Market there are still many old half-timbered houses. The visitor who follows the "Schar", a narrow alley connecting the two markets, can hardly see the sky between the ancient beams. A number of old patrician houses have survived the vicissitudes of time, among them the Dienheimer Hof with its charming Renaissance oriel window.

There is not much left of the old Kauzenburg of the Counts of Sponheim, but there is a particularly fine view of the city from the ruins of the castle. On the slopes above the city, in such locations as "Krötenpfuhl", "Narrenkappe", "Brückes" or "Schlossböckelheimer", grow wines that are among the best in the Nahegau.

"Little Venice" in Bad Kreuznach

Kreuznach's "Little Venice" is on the Ellerbach. The jumble of old houses crowded together face the water with an almost Latin casualness. Kreuznach's great and turbulent son, the painter Müller, especially loved this picturesque spot and the near-by "Zwickel", a little alley of old-time beauty. At the other end of the city is a particularly fine piece of Roman mosaic work, a tiled floor dating from the 3rd century A. D. Over half a million individual stones show in lively colors the games in a Roman amphitheater.

A last high spot in the Old Town are the bridge houses over the mill pond. Built high on narrow foundations, they and their reflections in the water are reminders of a more contemplative mediaeval world.

After the line of the Counts of Sponheim died out, the Margraves of Baden, the Counts of Simmern and the Count Electors Palatine shared the possession of Kreuznach. Shortly after this it became a seat of provincial administration in the Palatinate and remained so until occupied by Napoleon. In World War I it was the emperor's headquarters until the flood of January, 1918. During the last war a generation of medical doctors received training in Kreuznach's barracks and viewed the beauties of the Nahe valley with mixed feelings.

The foundation of the spa was laid by Hofrat Dr. Prieger when mineral springs containing radium were discovered. It was not until 1956 that the handsome Kurhaus could be fully used again for its original purpose. During the last two decades Kreuznach has become one of the leading radium spas and successfully treats rheumatism, women's diseases, children's diseases and chronic bronchial troubles.

A massif with steep, almost alpine porphyry cliffs lies to the north of *Bad Münster*. Before the Nahe forces its way through towards Kreuznach it takes time to form a lake at Rheingrafenstein, which is today a playground for boats and swans. As early as the 15th century salt was produced in Münster. The Rheingrafen spring is the warmest in the whole valley. During the last war the watering place was almost completely destroyed, but it has experienced a rapid recovery during the last decade. The curative powers of its springs are similar to those of Kreuznach.

For centuries the knights of Rheingrafenstein Castle were the owners of the town. The Rhinegrafen, or Counts on the Rhine, loyally supported the Counts of Sponheim in their feud with the Bishop of Mainz. Johann von Sponheim barely escaped the bishop's troops in the battle of Sprendlingen thanks to the brave action of the Kreuznach butcher, Michel Mort, while Rheingraf Siegfried was captured, enduring hard imprisonment and losing part of his lands. Mediaeval knights showed courage and steadfastness, but the chance of fortune alone determined whether loyalty should be rewarded. In 1689 the castle on the rocky height was destroyed by the French.

Between the valleys of the Nahe and the Alsenz rises *Ebernburg* Castle, the ancestral seat of the Sickingens and Hutten's famous "Inn of Justice". In the years of his fame Franz von Sickingen here received the emissaries of the nobles and the German emperor, but also messengers from Luther and the French King. In Ebernburg Castle not only Hutten but Kaspar Aquila, Johann Schweblin, Martin Butzer and other supporters of the Reformation found refuge. After the knight's sudden death they had to flee. The Count Electors of the Palatinate and Trier and the Landgrave of Hesse saw to it that this wasps' nest was thoroughly destroyed.

In the valley of the Alsenz steep flat-topped mountains repeatedly force the river and the road to make sharp bends. On the end of a ridge the stronghold *Altenbaumburg* commands the valley on two sides, a huge curtain-wall protecting it from attack from the east. Until the end of the 15th century the Raugrafen were lords of the castle. According to legend, one of the counts, returning from the Crusades, in a fit of blind jealousy murdered his wife and her page. His ghost is said to have long appeared at night in the castle courtyard and where the deed took place two white lilies blossomed. The line is long since extinct and the castle fallen into decay, but the old people down in the valley tell the story with as much feeling as though they or their immediate forebears had themselves witnessed the crime.

The old town hall of the wine-growing town of *Alsenz* rests on massive arches. The Alsenz wines from "Elkersberg" and "Sonnenberg" and the Traminer have absorbed the sunlight and spicy fragrance of the Palatinate. Lovely paths through the woods lead from here to the Donnersberg, the highest mountain in the Palatinate. Kirchheimbolanden in the fertile northern Palatinate is not far away and a visit to the once fortified town is well worth while. The mansion in Empire style of the well-known family of von Gienanth in Eisenberg is also worth a visit.

The keep of the stronghold *Landsberg* looms up in the distance long before we reach the little town of *Obermoschel*. Near the castle is an old quicksilver mine, once mentioned by Goethe in his travel notes, which was in operation until the last century. Great masses of ruins show the castle to have been one of the strongest in the country. It passed from the knights of Schmiedberg to the Counts of Veldenz and through marriage to the Palatinate Wittelsbachs. Today the imagination can picture the extent of the huge structure and the elaborate princly court. In 1689 the castle, the pride of the Dukes of Zweibrücken, was razed by the French and left to decay.

Vineyards follow along the south slopes till Meisenheim. The road passes near one of the oldest centers of Christianity in the country. The beginnings of the monastery of Disibodenberg, as of the monastery of Hornbach near Zweibrücken, go back to the earliest years of the 8th century, a whole generation earlier than the better known Benedictine abbey of Lorsch near Bensheim!

Meisenheim receives its visitors with the pictureque Lower Tower on the Glan. The streets and byways of the city offer many opportunities to admire the homes of nobles or townsmen with their elaborate half-timber work. A particular gem is the town hall with its high pointed arches and the lovely Renaissance oriel window. Towards the west the old city wall with its loopholes and defenses runs along behind the houses.

The Magdalene Building with its beautiful staircase tower is all that remains of the castle of the Dukes of Zweibrücken. Here in 1689 the Countess Palatine Charlotte Friederike saved the city from destruction through her intercession with the French, as Duchess Luise Juliane had done fifty years earlier when the city was threatened by the emperor's troops.

The largest church on the Glan is the collegiate church in Meisenheim. A covered path connects the old commandery of the Order of Knights of St. John with the churchyard. The ground plan and the distribution of masses show the influence of Nuremberg builders. The finest part of the interior is the burial chapel with its double vaulting. With what playful lightness, of which only the Gothic was capable, are the threads of the double network woven together! The lower network – with what sureness did the builder proceed! – is freely suspended. Those interested in tracing musical elements in the extravagant lines of the late Gothic, need merely look above them in the burial chapel at Meisenheim.

By way of Lauterecken, once seat of a branch line of the Dukes of Zweibrücken, the road leads to *Offenbach* on the Glan. The Benedictine church of the town is one of the most important buildings showing the transitional style between Romanesque and Gothic. The power of the Romanesque is not yet broken; horizontal lines are still important. The splendid pillars in the choir – excellently reproduced in a picture in this book – and the niches in the crossing are still wholly in the spirit of the late Romanesque. But above the capitals the new era begins. The arches soar upwards and meet at a sharp angle.

It is probable that the builder came from Champagne, brought here through the Remigius monastery near Kusel, which belonged to Rheims. With great care he tried to harmonize the old and the new architecture. He was satisfied with an octagonal tower at the crossing. In the vaulting, however, he bent and stretched the pillars and ribs, as he had been accustomed to do in France, and his windows are also higher and narrower.

As the head of an old monastic order, the abbot who had the church built doubtless wanted to follow tradition. And so two different periods have met in Offenbach and in their proximity have not disturbed one another. In the end the monk may have looked at the choir and the builder at his vaults and windows, and each may have been in his way satisfied.

Kusel, an important center in the Westrich region, lies around a sharp bend of the Glan in a deep cup-shaped valley. In the early middle ages the town belonged to the Remigius monastery, and with it to Rheims. Gradually the Counts of Veldenz as bailiffs of the monastery gained influence and finally they erected *Lichtenberg* Castle in defiance of the monastery. The emperor conceded the justice of the Abbot's complaint, but the weakness of the Holy Roman Empire prevented enforcement of the decision.

The counts and their successors, the Dukes of Zweibrücken, added to Lichtenberg till it was the largest castle in the Palatinate. Behind bushes the entrance tower with its opening for pouring pitch awaits the enemy. Through the deep apertures of the horseshoe-shaped tower canon could at any time be fired in all directions. A picturesque part of the great fortress is the second entrance tower with the former Landschreiberei or county clerk's office. A fine picture in this book shows the view from there.

Of the lower and older castle only the walls are left. The chapel was not added till the eighteenth century. The shafts of the cisterns extended down to the floor of the valley. Lichtenberg, a favorite residence of the Dukes of Zweibrücken, was never laid waste by an enemy. A fire, starting in a tithe barn, largely destroyed the castle and the work was completed by people of the region to whom the ruin was a convenient and inexpensive stone quarry. And yet enough has survived to testify to the high level of the mediaeval science of fortification in the Palatinate.

Offweiler Hof near Zweibrücken

In the Zweibrücken Country

The road leads us to the furthest tip of the Westrich region. In the old crown lands of the Merovingians the Counts of Saarbrücken established a custom-house and thereby laid the foundations for the city of *Zweibrücken*. The city has experienced many changes in the course of history. As bailiffs of the monastery of Hornbach, the Counts of Saarbrücken, like the Counts of Leiningen and Veldenz, were eager to bring the secular possessions of the monastery under their control. In 1353 Zweibrücken was made a city together with Hornbach. Soon after this the counts sold the city to the Count Electors Palatine.

The independent collateral line of the Dukes of Zweibrücken arose following a division of the country among heirs. Soon the Dukes took a leading place after the Count Electors in the Reichstag, and later through the Birkenfeld branch of the family became the ancestors of all the Wittelsbachs. The pastor Johannes Schweblin, a follower of von Hutten, whom we have already met with in Ebernburg Castle, introduced the Protestant faith here with the help of Duke Ludwig II. The monastery of Hornbach protested vigorously, but a public disputation held by its defender, Magister Kaltenhäuser, was of no avail. During the Thirty Years War the Duchy was a close ally of France. Reinhold von Rosen, who successfully defended the city against the imperial forces, died a Marshall of France.

Three Swedish kings were descended from the Zweibrücken line, and under Karl XII the Duchy even became a Swedish province. Count Oxenstierna administered the country more prudently than many of the native rulers. Under the architect Sundahl elements of the Swedish Renaissance mingled with Zweibrücken Baroque, giving it its distinctive character. Adventurous figures, such as Stanislaus Leszcinski, once king of Poland by grace of Karl XII, lived in the city. Leszcinski soon had to flee to Alsace and saw only the beginnings of his country-seat Tschifflik. As a favorite of Louis XIV he later succeeded in becoming Duke of Lorraine-truly a remarkable career for this agile Baroque potentate.

Zweibrücken was a Baroque city, the Salzburg of the Palatinate. The Residence and the heart of the city, the buildings in the Herzogsvorstadt, or Duke's suburb, numerous country seats in the surroundings, as well as Guttenbrunnen Castle, were all stamped with the spirit of this period. In the Residence were paintings, rugs and faience of the same Baroque period.

Karlsberg Castle was the most daring building project of the Palatinate Wittelsbachs. The western front extended for over a thousand meters, and lights gleamed in the evening from hundreds of windows. The park, Karlslust, contained exotic plants and animals. Knigge, who was able to approach the buildings unhindered, marveled at it and called Karlsberg a fairy castle.

But no laughter of a merry company echoed through its rooms, much as they would have been suited for it. In its festive halls no courtiers heard concerts or danced a graceful minuet. Like one of his successors, Ludwig II of Bavaria, Duke Karl August shut himself off from the world. He wanted to enjoy his residence, the fulfilment of his dreams, alone, and regarded every attempt to approach it as a serious and punishable disturbance.

Thus only a few guests, among them Emperor Joseph II, had a chance to admire the buildings. In 1794 the Duke had to leave his castle and flee from the approaching French and the victor made quick work of the destruction of this marvel of creation. The visitor today has difficulty finding even a trace of it in the landscape east of Homburg.

On the evening of March 14, 1945, Baroque Zweibrücken was reduced to rubble and ashes. Of the beautiful heart of the city little remained standing. Great efforts have been made in rebuilding to preserve the spirit of the past. The Alexander Church again towers up above the roofs of the city, but the famous late Gothic reticulated valuting was unfortunately destroyed in the air raid. There is a delightful staircase tower at the entrance. The ascent to the princes' seat and the tracery of the gallery show the high level of Zweibrücken filigree work. Numerous tombstones of the dukes remind one that the Alexander Church was both court and burial church.

On the west side of the Castle Square the archives building is still standing. Of the Baroque Residence itself only a blackened torso remains. The Rococo houses of the Duke's suburb have suffered the least damage. A picture in this book shows a part of Guttenbrunnen Castle which has been preserved.

Meanwhile a new, modern Zweibrücken, planned with a clarity worthy of its great past, has arisen. Even the famous rose-garden has increased in size. Practically all existing sorts of roses are to be found in its carefully tended flower beds, when they are in blossom a real paradise, not only for flower lovers.

One of the oldest Christian settlements in the country is the monastery of *Hornbach* on the road to Bitsch. The founder of the monastery of Reichenau, St. Pirmin, at the beginning of the 8th century founded here his tenth and last monastery. Only a few years ago his grave was found and a chapel erected over the ancient walls. During the last war the cloister – hidden for centuries by farmhouses – and the old Fabian convent were found and cleared of obstructions. On the street the Romanesque south tower of the monastery is still standing among roofs.

For some centuries the venerable Fabian convent had to take the shape of a farmhouse and one of the oldest crypts in the country served as a potato cellar. The stone monk at the end of the round arch that supports the vaulting of the crypt was protected from complete destruction by the accumulation of soil over the centuries. The tombstones and endstones of the crypt, however, were victims of the farmer's potato cart. One sees only where they fitted in. The farmer's kitchen is in the side chapel of the transept. Here one can truly say that the centuries meet! Where the plaster has fallen away one can see the old round arches by the new windows, and it is not hard to imagine how they formerly ended. The southern part of the convent is not as old and the style indicates the 11th or 12th century.

The Romanesque builders knew how to make walls! The masonry is exactly put together and the mortar of astonishing hardness. On the other hand, the farmer's walls already show cracks and have to be propped up. Here one sees clearly that the farmer was building for generations, the monk, however, was preparing for eternity.

In the convent yard are the old monks' graves. The stone coffins were made with a special place left for the head, as a picture in this book shows. The gravestones over them were firmly fastened down, so that when the coffins were opened a few years ago, the bones of the monks lay untouched by time in the same position in which they had been placed in the grave. Over a thousand years of silence had passed over them.

In the Heart of the Palatinate

Pirmasens, as its name betrays, is one of the oldest settlements founded by St. Pirmin's monastery, Hornbach. It would always have remained a small place if it had not been for Landgrave Ludwig and his grenadiers. The quiet village became a drill ground and rapidly grew into a city. "Little Prussia" in the Palatinate was fortunately never involved in a serious war. The Hessian treasury paid the "tall fellows" such a small salary that the soldiers' wives early had to look around for some additional source of income. From used sword-belts and other materials procured from the court they began to make house-shoes, called in the Palatinate "Schlappen", which were soon popular articles at near-by markets. After the Landgrave's death this new occupation helped many families to survive and became the nucleus of the Pirmasens shoe industry. Some of the soldiers also opened booths at fairs and their descendants have their stands today wherever there is "Kerwe", or annual fair, in the Palatinate.

Like most Palatinate cities, Pirmasens has had its ups and downs. But the tenacity and vitality of the inhabitants have helped the city and the shoe manufacture flourish again after each set-back. The descendants of the grenadiers have remained the backbone of the constantly growing shoe industry. Badly hit in World War I and even more so in World War II, Pirmasens has nevertheless been able to maintain its position as a leading city in the shoe industry and its sample fairs are important for the European market.

Kaiserslautern's paradise for bathers at Gelterswoog, surrounded by woods, is the largest and probably finest bathing beach in the Palatinate. On a near-by height is *Hohenecken* Castle, once

Pirmasens

the south-western bastion to guard Emperor Barbarossa's palace. This important stronghold was in the 12th century already in the possession of the knights of Lautern; of this family, Eberhard was a governor in Italy and Heinrich von Lautern was court marshal of the Hohenstaufen emperors. Beyond these ruined walls lies Vogelsweh, a new-world island in the midst of the old world and the largest American settlement on the European continent. "Little America" seems to go on and on in the belt of woods by Kaiserslautern. Many streets radiate and through the trees countless homes, storehouses and barracks can be seen. The visitor must make many stops for traffic before reaching the heart of the city.

Kaiserslautern lies at a crossroad, where the old Kings' Highway and the almost equally old road from Mainz to Pirmasens intersect. This highway from east to west has lost none of its importance in the present day.

Little is left of either Lutra, the court of the Frankish kings, or the Hohenstaufen imperial palace. What remains of them has found a place in the famous Burgmuseum, or castle museum, together with the foundations of the Renaissance castle of Count Palatine Casimir. Only the collegiate church which Emperor Barbarossa erected for the Premonstratensians looms up as it always has above the roofs of the city. With its splendor and the majesty of its proportions, it is one of the most important examples in the Palatinate of the Gothic hall church, where aisles and nave are the same height.

The slopes of the Palatine Forest around Kaiserslautern were long the scene of the old legend of the sleeping emperor in the hollow mountain. The story is of the longed-for return of the Hohenstaufen Emperor Friedrich II, who was able without help from an army to force the German princes and his own rebellious son to do homage to him. German noblemen, Arabian scholars and Moorish warriors gathered around him in Sicily. The Holy Land and Jerusalem fell to him almost without fighting, like a ripe fruit. The whole Occident looked to him as he signed an important treaty in the tent of the Sultan of Egypt. In the confusion of the period without a king that soon followed, Friedrich II became a symbolic figure of the German emperor as such. Centuries passed before the figure of his grandfather, Friedrich Barbarossa, who had a personal connection with this region, gradually took his place in the legend. As late as the 16th century it was said that a huge carp had been caught in the "Kaiserswoog", with a golden ring in its mouth and a chain with Greek letters, which had been put in the pool by Emperor Friedrich.

Kaiserslautern, declared a free imperial city by Rudolf von Habsburg in 1276, came into the possession of the Counts Palatine one hundred years later. The city suffered greatly during the Thirty Years War; barely a tenth of the population survived the terrible storming of the city by Croatians. In 1793, after winning the battle of Kaiserslautern, the Prussians were able to drive the French out of the region temporarily. The center of the struggle was the "Galgenschanze" or "gallows redoubt", where today is located the main plant of the well-known firm Pfaff.

Kaiserslautern is a city of woods. All around its walls within easy reach lie the slopes of the Palatine Forest. For over five hundred years the town council and citizens have every ten years walked in procession around the boundaries of the city woods. Formerly the boys were laid over the "Jungfernstein" and given a beating, a somewhat drastic method of impressing upon the next generation where the city boundaries ran in the valuable forest.

Landstuhl, like Kaiserslautern formerly a residence of the Frankish kings, also lies on the old Kings' Highway to Saarbrücken. In Nanstein Castle Franz von Sickingen, besieged by the rulers of Trier, Hesse and the Palatinate, was killed by an enemy bullet. His sons later erected a memorial stone in his honor and enlarged the fortress to a Renaissance castle. The tombstone, with an impressive portrait of the knight in relief, may be seen in the Catholic parish church. The castle was destroyed in that year of terror, 1689. Landstuhl itself, whose walls formerly connected it with Nanstein Castle, has grown and extends into the surrounding moors, a region formerly regarded with fear.

Only a few miles east of Kaiserslautern lies the well-known monastery church of Enkenbach. It is not hard to distinguish the various periods that have contributed to the structure. The side aisle to the south is noticeably lower, as though the monastery had not enough money left to continue paying the builder's salary. The most important and best-known part of the church is the main portal. Here the "vineyard of the Church" is represented in rich and elaborate late Romanesque ornament. With the greatest care the Palatine masons have hewed vines with all sorts of little animals from the stone. At both sides – still in the spirit of the early middle ages – on the springing-stones dragons guard the entrance.

By way of Mehlingen one can quickly reach the most important church in the heart of the Palatinate. In *Otterberg* as elsewhere the Cistercians, true to their principles, built the monastery on the floor of a valley. Originally many monastery farm buildings must have stood around the great church of yellow sandstone. In keeping with the spirit of Cistercian clarity, ornament has been used sparingly on the Romanesque-early Gothic walls. Only at the entrance and in the great rose-window of the west front did the monks make use of more flowing and graceful outlines. How strictly the purity of line was preserved even in the gradation of the 16 pillars at the main portal, can be clearly seen in a beautiful photograph in this book.

In Otterberg Romanesque and early Gothic elements intermingle. The church was built in a relatively short time – only three generations of masons worked here – so that it has a high degree of unity. No building far and near can compare in beauty and in the clarity of its exterior with this old monastery church.

The Palatine Forest and the Wasgau

The Palatine Forest, Germany's largest nature reservation, is one of the few oases of quiet and seclusion that is left us. Here the hustle and bustle of everyday life seem far away. An unaccustomed stillness lies over the valleys and pastures; here and there one meets with a wagon loaded with logs. Only on the bigger highways is one reminded of the motor age and one can walk for days along forest paths through the mountains without meeting anyone. On longer walking trips one can follow trails marked by the Pfälzerwald-Verein (the Palatine Forest Club) in many directions.

What a variety of views! The sandstone soil gleams red as fire through the trees. In the spring yellow broom mingles with the young green of the beechwoods. In the fall heather with its purplish-blue blossoms borders the paths through woods bright with autumnal colors. The widespread tops of the pines suggest those of southern climes. Near "Johanniskreuz", the watershed between the Rhine and the Moselle, stand huge old trees, great masses of foliage. Numerous ancient castle ruins crown the mountain-tops.

Karlstal is a particularly beautiful spot, especially where the valley narrows to a gorge, and a walk beside the rushing waters of the Moosalb is well worth while. One should turn off along the narrow road to Schmalenberg, where gentle hills, meadows with ponds, and wooded slopes seem to breathe peace. The drive from Johanniskreuz down to Annweiler or Merzalben is also beautiful. And then the road to the summit of the *Kalmit!* It winds its way up in a series of hairpin curves, while glimpses of the plain and of the side valleys constantly tempt one to stop. From this mountain, the second highest in the Palatinate, there are magnificent views in all directions. The descent to Elmstein is like that from a pass, with abrupt drops and adventurous curves, the trees meeting above the road to form an arch. *Elmstein, Trippstadt* and other villages in this region are favorite vacation spots for lovers of quiet.

The Modenbach valley, on the other hand, reminds one of alpine foothills. Large herds of cattle graze in meadows bordered by tall firs. Up on the Steigerkopf one should not fail to take the short walk to the "Schänzel", a lookout tower which was erected as a memorial to those who fell in the year 1794. From here one has a panoramic view of the entire Palatine Forest. To the north long ridges stretch towards the Donnersberg, while nearby is the still higher Kalmit. To the south one sees the confused outlines of the mountain ranges in the Wasgau, with the Trifels standing out against the background of the Vosges mountains. On the private road from the forester's lodge at Heldenstein to Taubensuhl the visitor is completely surrounded by woods which in variety of form and stillness seem like a primeval forest. But the footpath to Taubensuhl, always following the red markings, is even lovelier.

The most attractive part of the Palatinate as regards landscape is the *Wasgau*. Mountains of varied shapes, some flat-topped, others conical, some side by side, others before or behind them, form a lively picture, interspersed with ridges of gentler contours. No two views are alike. Not without reason is the Wasgau sometimes called the "Palatine Switzerland". Faults in the sandstone have led to the creation of fantastic rock formations which are irregularly scattered on the mountain slopes like big red toadstools. Around the resort *Dahn* they are so numerous that people speak of the Dahn cliff country. Popular imagination has given each cliff its name, such as for instance the "Devil's Table" near Hinterweidenthal (shown in this volume), the "Maiden's Leap" or the "Bride and Groom" near Dahn, and many others.

One of the loveliest views in the Wasgau is that from the ruins of *Lindelbrunn* Castle. A narrow road brings one nearly to the top of the mountain. To the north rises the Trifels group with the Asselstein, a favorite place for practicing alpine climbing. A sharp peak to the northeast is the Hundsfelsen, which can only be scaled through a dangerous chimney. To the south the Rödelstein and the Puhlstein form a picturesque foreground. The view embraces large parts of the Dahn cliff country. In the Wasgau most of the castles are built into cliffs. Passages and casemates cut into the rock connect the outworks with each other. The best known cliff castles are Altdahn, Drachenfels, the Wegelnburg and especially *Berwartstein* Castle. In the last-named a steep tubular rock chimney formed the entrance and made the castle impervious to attack. Berwartstein is one of the few castles in the Palatinate that has been rebuilt. A remarkable feature is the underground system of passages in the rock. The well, with a diameter of two meters, is 100 meters deep, reaching to the floor of the valley! The castle acquired a sinister fame when it was occupied by the robber baron Hans von Drodt, called Trapp. Even today in the Wasgau naughty children are warned to "be good or Hans Trapp will get you!"

King of the castles in the Wasgau, however, is the *Trifels!* On neighboring peaks lie the strongholds Anebos and Scharfenberg, which belong to the Trifels group. Trifels was an important Hohenstaufen imperial fortress, as one can see from the strength of the old chapel tower. In times of stress the imperial crown jewels were brought here for safekeeping. No less a person that the English king, Richard Coeur de Lion, was imprisoned within its walls. The residential building with the imperial hall has been rebuilt according to old models and its interior gives one a vivid impression of the spacious rooms of the Hohenstaufen period.

At the foot of the Trifels lies the charming little town of *Annweiler*. Many half-timbered houses border the pretty market place. An attractive walk is that along the Queich, ending at an old mill wheel. Annweiler owes the fact that it was made a city to its protector, the last great Hohenstaufen emperor, Friedrich II.

Neustadt

Along the German Wine Highway

A sea of grapevines bearing great names surrounds the villages along the Haardt. From the time of the first spring sunshine the one care of the wine-growers is for the development of the vines. If they are threatened by cold at the time of the ice-saints (Pancratius, Servatius, Bonifatius and Sophia, whose days occur around the middle of May, when late frosts are common), the vineyards between Neustadt and Kallstadt and in many places in the Oberhaardt are aglow with little stoves. In the most important vineyards, like Deidesheimer Kieselberg, Forster Ungeheuer or Kallstadter Saumagen, the fires are so close together that the passer-by at night can read a newspaper by their light and not feel the cold. Even the famous highway has to take into account the location of the vineyards. Turning and twisting, often on the edge of the vineyards, it winds its way slowly northwards. The experience of centuries determines the location of the vineyards. For example, Impflingen, though not near the Wine Highway, has for a thousand years produced good wines, as the Implinger "Heide" proves. Looking down from the mountains and castles of the Haardt, one can follow the boundaries of the wine belt. From the Madenburg or the Maxburg one can clearly see the increase in the vineyard area and the villages in the Mittelhaardt. To speak of the wines of the Palatinate is, for the gourmet, to luxuriate in the higher levels of enjoyment! The Palatinate wine is not drunk as lightly as the aristocrat from the Rheingau nor does it affect the lower extremities like the growths from Baden with their earthy aroma. In contrast to the Moselle wines it has left its youth behind – but not its youthfulness – and has developed beyond the agreeable wines of Rheinhesse. It is more masculine than its brothers to the north and has more balance and warmth than its southern neighbors.

The Palatinate wine leads to that exhilaration of the senses that gives courage to the timorous, arouses ardor in the phlegmatic, and makes the quiet drinker enthusiastic. It has fullness and in some wines from Forst a body that demands of the connoisseur that he hold his own like a man. Enjoyed in the right quantities, it creates enchantment and intoxication of the soul without detriment to the body. No other wine offers such a wide skala of tastes. It is sound, sunny and has elegance; its masculine succulence is never merely agreeable, and its quality convinces, whether or not it may have won prizes.

The wines of the Oberhaardt are the right preparation for the great names between Neustadt and Bad Dürkheim. Especially good are those from Schweigen, Edenkoben, Maikammer or St. Martin. The guest who stops for a meal at the Leinweiler Hof will choose a Siebeldinger, Frankweiler or Rhodter to enjoy with his good dinner. Or if he orders one of the famous omelettes with mushrooms at the Winzergenossenschaft Dalberg in St. Martin, he will afterwards drink with satisfaction a Spätlese of Dalberger Riesling. The average wines of the Oberhaardt are better than the best of some other regions, even though they do not have top rating in the skala of Palatinate wines.

The landscape of the great Palatinate wines is the Mittelhaardt from Neustadt to Bad Dürkheim. Neustadter, Gimmeldinger and Mussbacher vineyards give a first promise of what is to come. And then the Deidesheimer! No other German wine can compare with it if the vintage has been able to absorb enough sunshine. The smooth elegance of a Kieselberg, a Hofstück or a Leinhöhle, to name just a few, their prickling freshness and the desire one has to laugh from pure pleasure after each sip – no other wine can produce quite the same effect. This seductive Deidesheimer is the aristocratic peak of Palatinate wines. After tasting one of its sunny vintages, the visitor is drawn back to the famous town again and again.

It is just a stone's throw from here to Forst, with its wines of noble ripeness, more contemplative and less exhuberant than those of Deidesheim. The full-bodied Forster Spätlese seems to contain a bit of the ancient wisdom that reconciles one to the inevitability of growing older. When they have reached their third glass of Forster Ungeheuer or Jesuitengarten, old and young are ready to compose verses, which, however, they rarely put down on paper, as that would interrupt their drinking. The guest who drinks Forster at "Spindler's" or at the Winzergenossenschaft drifts imperceptibly from hour to hour into a world of far-ranging contemplation.

The wines of Bad Dürkheim, whether from the "Michelsberg", "Spielberg" or other vineyards, already foreshadow the qualities that distinguish the wines further north. Names like Ungsteiner "Honigsäckel" (literally "honey bag") and Herxheimer "Himmelreich" ("heaven") suggest a milder, sweeter growth. These lack perhaps the warm undertones, the distinction and fine differences of Deidesheimer or Forster, but the northern Mittelhaardt wines, especially the Kallstadter, are soft, agreeable to the palate and not light. Before enjoying a Kallstadter "Saumagen" one is well advised to eat a hearty meal. In Henninger's famous Saumagen Weinstube guests are served not only wine from the best vineyards but delicious culinary specialties.

Let no one underestimate the Unterhaardt wines! In Grünstadt, Klein-Karlbach, Bockenheim and Neuleiningen there grows a highly presentable Riesling.

After this little excursion among the joys of wine, let us return to the southern part of the Wine Highway. In *Schweigen* the great Wine Gate looks towards Alsace. The Schweigener Gewürztraminer, fresh, sturdy and most agreeable to drink, strikes the opening note. After a good glass of it our way takes us on to *Dörrenbach*, a little mediaeval town surrounded by a forest of chestnut trees. The fortified cemetery, with its loop-holes and towers, is a curiosity and the only one of its kind in the Palatinate. After the destruction of Guttenberg Castle, the cemetery became a bastion first for the Princes of Leiningen, later for the Princes of Zweibrücken. In 1460 it withstood five attacks by Palatinate troops. The dead of friend or foe had not far to go to their last resting place. On this weekend a notice fastened to the side gate of the cemetery announced that the "hoof trimmer" would be in the village on the coming Monday. The town hall in Dörrenbach is one of the finest half-timbered buildings in the Palatinate. The elaborate woodcarving of its Renaissance stairs and the old cemetery are pictured in this book.

Bergzabern is the real gateway to the Wasgau. The castle with its attractive Baroque corner towers recalls the days when the city belonged to the Dukes of Zweibrücken. The former bailiff's house, now the "Gasthaus zum Engel", is the finest Renaissance dwelling house in the Palatinate. Bergzabern has become very popular as a resort for taking a "Kneipp" cure; the spa with its carefully tended park lies amidst woods to the west of the city, a restful spot and the starting point of many walks.

By way of Pleisweiler and the pretty wine-growing village of Gleiszellen we reach *Klingenmünster*, the birthplace of the well-known poet August Becker. All that remains of the old Benedictine monastery is the Romanesque west tower. Half way up the hillside, between the ruins of the Leiningen stronghold Landeck and the town, lie the St. Nicholas chapel and the Magdalenenhof. The little church with its Romanesque and Gothic arches is a peaceful spot. At the entrance is a sign in big letters requesting the visitor to wipe his feet before taking the big wrought-iron key from the little box where it is kept.

From the ruins of the *Madenburg* above Eschbach the view ranges from Heidelberg and Speyer to Strassburg; to the southwest is spread out the diversified panorama of the Wasgau mountains, as a picture in this book shows.

Landau's strategic position on the Queich River has sometimes meant hardship for the city. For the French kings the city was long a thorn in the flesh, since its situation where the route over the pass from Zweibrücken crossed the old Roman road to Strassburg made it a threat to the southern part of their dominions. During the Thirty Years War it changed hands probably oftener than any other place in the Palatinate. Finally the city became French for more than a century and under Vauban was strongly fortified. Its citizens experienced and celebrated the French Revolution and shortly afterwards witnessed the terror of the guillotine, which was set up in the Paradeplatz. "Landau ou la mort" was a battle-cry of the young republic for which many had to die.

The old collegiate church shows no signs of these troubled times. The stately structure testifies to Landau's importance in the middle ages and frescoes in the 14th century sacristy show the visitor that notable painters must have stayed in the city. The graceful contours of the Augustinian church strike a harmonious note. Its Gothic cloister seems to have preserved a trace of the stillness which must once have reigned in the monastic seclusion within its walls.

The Rhine at Germersheim

Landau is one of the most important towns in the Vorderpfalz and shares with Speyer and Neustadt a leading position in the wine trade. Whether or not he is himself a wine drinker, the visitor will find the Wine Museum well worth seeing.

Nearby is Bellheim, home of the "Bellemer Heiner", writer of verses and songs in dialect which are popular throughout the Palatinate. The portly mayor, a friend of the poet's, has introduced the custom of the handsel, a sum of money given by the village authorities to newly married couples. From here it is only a short distance to *Germersheim,* the old strongly fortified city, Rudolf von Habsburg's last stopping place before his death. A quarrel about this fortress was the immediate cause of the destructive War of the Palatinate Succession and brought General Mélac, that scourge of the Palatinate, into the country.

After passing through the wine-growing villages of Albersweiler and Frankenweiler and Bad Gleisweiler, where sanitoriums have been built to take advantage of the favorable climate, the visitor is tempted to stop for a glass of "Schäwer" in the Ritterstube in Burrweiler. In Rhodt, too, one may wish to stop at the Schlössel, or "Little Castle", for a taste of the well-known Traminer, drunk in a picture gallery. From another wine-growing village, Weyher, on the edge of the Haardt forest, one has a particularly fine view. After a few glasses of "Edenkobener Kirchberg" or "Klostergut", what could be pleasanter than to float by chair lift to the top of the Rietburg, from which one has a wide panorama of the plain.

At the foot of the Haardt mountains lies the picturesque wine-growing village of *St. Martin.* When approached from the breathtaking descent from the high Kalmit, the valley suddenly opens out at the end of the Totenkopfstrasse, the roofs and church tower emerge from the gentle contours of the vineyards, and the pleasant expanse of the Rhine plain stretches out on each side. Coming from the forest ravines, the wanderer finds the friendly vineyard landscape somehow reassuring. The figure of St. Martin, surrounded by vines, looks down from the churchyard wall. In the parish church there are a number of notable carvings, among them the sepulture of Christ (from about 1520) and a handsome double tombstone of the family of Dalberg, who were for a long time lords of the nearby Kropsburg. No visitor to the Palatinate should miss St. Martin!

In both Maikammer and Diedesfeld there are quite a few older houses to admire. There are numerous inns, too, so that the visitor has plenty of opportunity to taste his way through the various vineyards.

The great walls of *Hambach* Castle (also called the Maxburg or, because of the surrounding chestnut forests, "Kästeburg") proclaim from afar that it was one of the most important strongholds in the Palatinate. As early as the end of the 11th century the Salian line gave the castle to the cathedral chapter of Speyer, in whose hands it remained till the French Revolution. Like Altleiningen Castle, the Maxburg was burned in the Peasants War. The not very successful restoration under the Wittelsbachs, not even fully completed, could not rob the castle of its proud

Seebach Monastery

dignity. The curtain wall to protect the main residential building is two meters thick. Witness to the former strategic value of the fortress are the tremendous outer walls defiantly facing the plain. As a ruin the castle once more acquired historical importance through the "Hambacher Fest". At a critical time in 1832, 20,000 people from all parts of Germany, including the Heidelberg Burschenschaften (patriotic student associations), came together here under the black-red-gold flag in support of the ideal of a new, free Germany. In Hambach's inns, over a glass of the renowned Riesling, the visitor can hear winegrowers tell of all that happened in the castle in great-grandfather's time.

Neustadt on the Wine Highway was a residence of the Counts Palatine. Thanks to Palatine industriousness the city flourished, as one can see from the handsome dwelling houses in the Old Town and the more recent mansions on the hillside of the Haardt. The people of Neustadt always seem to have had luck on their side. In 1688 the city was occupied by the French but not burned, as were most of the Palatinate towns, and in the last war Neustadt suffered little damage.

The citizens of Neustadt in early times built a city they could well be proud of. The collegiate church takes up the whole side of the Rathausplatz and is considered one of the finest Gothic churches in the Palatinate. In the 14th century it was the burial place of the Counts Palatine on the Rhine. No other city in the Palatinate has a market place of such proportions or surrounded by such picturesque old buildings. Victor von Scheffel once stayed in a simple Renaissance house on the east side and the bookshop on the ground floor still bears his name. The Rathausplatz is surrounded by a maze of attractive little alleys and along the Speyerbach stand many old half-timbered houses.

In the 16th century Neustadt was the western center of the Reformed Church. Here Count Palatine Casimir founded his own university, when Heidelberg University refused to meet his wishes. It is one of the curiosities of history that the Casimirianum, the university building, later housed a Jesuit college.

No account of Neustadt would be complete without mention of its wines. Samples of the "Vogelsang", "Erkenbrecht" or "Klausenberg", to name just a few notable vineyards, are a pure delight, and not only to connoisseurs.

Gimmeldinger "Meerspinne", Mussbacher "Eselshaut" or "Königsbacher Jesuitengarten" herald the Deidesheimer wines and are related to them. At the foot of the beautiful town hall stairs in *Deidesheim* it is an old annual custom on Whit-Tuesday to auction off the Lambrecht goat, symbol of the early right of Lambrecht to pasturage in the Deidesheim forest. The famous wine-growing town was first mentioned in documents in 699 and received city rights towards the end of the 14th century. The former bishops' residence in the north-eastern part of the city in a reminder of the time when Deidesheim belonged to the cathedral chapter of Speyer. In the cellars of the famous wine estate v. Bassermann-Jordan stands a beautiful Gothic woodcarving of St. Urban, who, like St. Cyriak, is a patron saint of the winegrowers in this region.

The finest Gothic pulpit in the Palatinate is that in the parish church of the wine-growing village of *Ruppertsberg*. Those who want to dine well and dance while enjoying their Ruppertsberger "Linsenbusch", "Reiterpfad" or "Hoheburg" will do well to go with a well-filled purse to Motzenbacker's. The pretty staircase of the "Schlössel" and the Baroque buildings of the well-known wine estate Bühl must owe some of their charm to the magic of Forst wines.

The complicated history of the Palatinate is well illustrated by the fact that *Wachenheim* was at one time a possession of the Archbishops of Trier. The Wachtenburg, a stronghold of the Counts Palatine, was destroyed in the Peasants War. Real Palatine courage was shown by the Wachenheim innkeeper who dared to hold a drinking competition with the Abbot of Limburg, a man of redoubtable capacity. After numerous bottles had been drunk, the great man finally lay under the table and the innkeeper could look forward to his reward: the abbot had promised that if he were defeated the innkeeper's vineyards should be forever free from tithes. Besides the better known "Gerümpel" the guest should not forget the "Altenburg Riesling"! It can hold its own with the best Deidesheim wines. Wachenheim champagne too has an excellent reputation.

In *Bad Dürkheim* the glasses contain sharply contrasting liquids. While some are happily sipping their "Michelsberg", "Nonnengarten" and "Schenkenbohl" or the red "Feuerberg" at the restaurant built in the shape of a great cask, or at one of the many Weinstuben, others, in the interests of health, are with sour expressions emptying glasses of mineral water containing arsenic from the Max spring in the pump-room.

In the middle ages the Counts of Leiningen already built salt works here and, as in Kreuznach, the mineral springs have made Bad Dürkheim an important spa. The city has surpassed itself in the designing of the park surrounding the springs, with its artistic and varied vistas.

When the Dürkheim Wurstmarkt, or Sausage Fair, is held, people from all over the world come in throngs to celebrate the largest wine festival in the Palatinate. Nowadays probably few if any of the people at the stands know that the fair was originally held at the chapel of St. Michael on the Michelsberg in connection with a pilgrimage. In Seebach, a part of the city, as survivals of the Benedictine nunnery only the late Romanesque east choir and the octagonal tower of the crossing are still standing. The rooms where the abbess formerly lived are now occupied by the "Käsbüro", where gourmet and wine-lover will find all they could wish for.

Limburg Monastery

Altleiningen Castle

Above the Isenach valley lie the ruins of the monastery of *Limburg*, related architecturally to the cathedral in Speyer. Emperor Konrad II laid the foundation stones of both churches. The crypt and the greater part of the church date from the early Romanesque period, while in the choir there are doors with the pointed Gothic arch. Judging from what remains of the church, it must have been a Romanesque structure of large proportions which could be defended. The great transept which once rose like a curtain wall towards the open flank to the west must have served as a defense for the monks in times of stress.

When the Counts of Leiningen built the *Hardenburg* in the Isenach valley, in violation of their duty as bailiffs, they cut off the monastery from its hinterland and brought it to a great extent under their control. The Hardenburg is one of the largest and strongest castles in the country. Even the French general Mélac only succeeded in blowing up its outworks. One hundred years later the French revolutionary army completed the destruction. The entrance tower and cannon tower had walls four meters thick. Deep underground passages connected the outworks with the main part of the castle. The extensive structure contained among other things stables, a smithy, a bakehouse and even a bathhouse.

Ungsteiner "Herrenberg" and Leistadter "Kalkofen" prepare one for the peak wines of Kallstadt. That the monasteries of Weissenburg, Lorsch, Limburg and even the Cistercian Otterberg had their establishments in Kallstadt is proof enough that for centuries the wine there has been carefully cultivated.

In no other town in the Vorderpfalz, Neustadt excepted, have so many picturesque old buildings been preserved as in *Freinsheim*. Particularly delightful is a stroll along the old city wall. Numerous gatehouses arch across the narrow alley, their steps clinging to the protecting wall, their beams slightly bent by time. The iron gate to the east is a symbol of this little fortified town. The connoisseur quickly makes friends with Freinsheimer "Musikantenbuckel".

Neuleiningen, a picturesque little town on a hilltop with houses crowded together, suggests an Italian mountain village. From the castle at the summit one has a wide view of the plain as well as of the Leiningen valley with its many ponds. In the choir of the parish church are some excellent 15th century figures of the apostles carved in wood.

*Baroque entrance gate
of the Oberhof in Grünstadt*

No visitor should miss a drive through the quiet beauty of the Leiningen valley. Altleiningen Castle takes up a whole mountain ridge; the many windows along the front show that the counts were lovers of well-lighted rooms. In the inner courtyard is a Renaissance porch of especial beauty. The castle is surpassed in spaciousness and magnificence only by the residence of the Counts Palatine in Heidelberg.

In *Grünstadt* the Counts of Altleiningen lived in the Unterhof, the Counts of Neulingen in the Oberhof. At the entrance to the former stables (now Malthouse Schlichting), on each of the posts a mail coach is carved in bas-relief. At the "Unterhaardt Wine Competition" every year on the first Sunday in October, Grünstadter "Höllenpfad" always gets one of the first prizes. On the way to Frankenthal one must be sure to stop and see the Catholic parish church in Laumersheim; it contains a statue of St. Stanislaus Kostka which admirably demonstrates the Baroque ability to combine nobleness of spirit with warmth of expression. For centuries the Augustinian canon monastery set its imprint upon the city of *Frankenthal*. In the western facade of the building near the Rathausplatz two different periods meet in balanced harmony. The arches of the side aisles have a suggestion of a point at the apex. The main portal, however, is flanked by delicate graduated pillars in the late Romanesque style of the early 13th century. In the 16th century the rooms of the monastery gave shelter to members of the Reformed Church from various countries. Frankenthal formerly had Dutch, Walloon and German church congregations. The new settlers, with their skill in cloth manufacture, helped the city to greater economic importance. Frankenthal also rapidly became famous for its porcelain manufacture and at a later period for its printing-machine factory.

The youngest city in the Palatinate had its origin in the old earthworks along the Rhine. *Ludwigshafen* has kept its youthful élan. Unhesitatingly it goes about securing everything necessary for the welfare of a modern city. The largest inland port on the left bank of the Rhine stretches out for

*Western front
of the Augustinian canon monastery
in Frankenthal*

20 kilometers. Heavy industries, unwelcome in the older cities, receive all the room they need. The Badische Anilin- und Sodafabrik (BASF) is free to expand as far as it wishes from the Friesenheimer Strasse to the Rhine and in the suburb of Oppau. The same is true of the pharmaceutical works of the firm Knoll AG, the Dr. Raschig chemical plant or the Halberg machine factory. The Walzmühle is the largest flour mill in Germany.

The problems arising from the terrible destruction of the last war are being tackled with remarkable energy. In rebuilding the center of the city, the emphasis has been on suitability of the buildings for their purpose and on the monumental impressiveness of smooth surfaces.

In the 6th century *Speyer* was already the seat of a Frankish bishop. As a reminder of Roman rule the historical museum treasures an amphora dating from the 3rd century A.D. and still containing liquid wine. Speyer became a cathedral city under Emperor Konrad II, who is buried there in the crypt. Under Heinrich IV the church was enlarged to proportions far exceeding anything existing at that time. A daring innovation for that period was the vaulting of the Romanesque nave, a venture which was completely successful. A solution that in the Gothic period became a matter of course was undertaken here in Speyer with the traditional means and without changing height or width. In the entire Occident there is nothing that can be compared with it. Salian and Hohenstaufen emperors gave the city every possible protection. The great cathedral embodied their conception of greatness, strength and permanence untouched by time.

Speyer was also often chosen as a meeting place for the Reichstag of the Holy Roman Empire. It was here in 1526 that the supporters of Luther made their protest against King Ferdinand's decision, one of the decisive moments in the history of Protestantism.

Old prints show Speyer in all the magnificence of a great mediaeval city, with a bewildering array of towers, churches and defenses. Goethe's delicate sketch of the city from the year 1779 shows Speyer very much as it looks today. Between the two aspects lies the fateful destruction that included the whole Palatinate.

The proud old gate tower, the "Altpörtel", has survived as a record of 13th century Speyer. The cathedral is still the largest Romanesque church on the European continent. The eastern part has never been seriously damaged by the vicissitudes of time. In its crypt lie the coffins of German emperors and kings. The recent restoration has again given the nave its original simplicity of style. In this great building, where Bernhard of Clairvaux once summoned Christendom to the Crusades, one can still feel the power and strength of early mediaeval faith.

We have now reached the end of our journey through the Palatinate. It has led us from the Nahe to the Glan, from the Zweibrücken country to Kaiserslautern, through the Wasgau, then, at a leisurely pace, from one wine-growing village to the next, and finally to Speyer. In this age of restless travel to southern lands, it has been our aim to recall to those who read this book and look at its pictures a charming German landscape.

In the crypt of Speyer Cathedral

Idyllische Partie im Kurviertel von Bad Kreuznach
Idyllic scenery at spa-quarter of Bad Kreuznach
Partie idyllique au quartier des bains de Bad Kreuznach

Fluß-Panorama von Bad Kreuznach   *Riverside panorama of Bad Kreuznach*   *Panorama de la rivière près de Bad Kreuznach*

3

Die Ebernburg bei Münster am Stein (Huttens berühmte Herberge der Gerechtigkeit)

Ebernburg Castle near Münster am Stein (Huttens famous inn of justice)

Château d'Ebernburg près de Münster am Stein, célèbre auberge de la justice de Hutten

Fachwerk und Meisenbrunnen am Rapportierplatz in Meisenheim
Timber framework and titmouse fountain at Meisenheim Report Square
Bâtisses en cloisonnage et fontaine des mésanges à la Place des Rapports à Meisenheim

Flußlandschaft am Glan mit der Schloßkirche von Meisenheim
River-landscape at the Glan with Meisenheim Castle-church
Paysage fluvial aux bords du Glan avec l'église du château à Meisenheim

Altenbaumburg mit Ausblick in das Alsenztal
Altenbaumburg with view into Alsenz valley
Château d'Altenbaumburg avec vue dans la vallée de l'Alsenz

Zweiter Eingangsturm mit Landschreiberei der Burg Lichtenberg bei Kusel
Second entrance-tower with county-chancellery of Lichtenberg Castle near Kusel
Seconde tour d'entrée avec chancellerie du pays du château Lichtenberg près de Kusel

9

Alte Mönchsgräber am Fabiansstift in Hornbach bei Zweibrücken

Old monk's graves along Fabian's monastery at Hornbach near Zweibrücken

Vieux tombeaux de moines le long du couvent de Fabian à Hornbach près de Zweibrücken

Spätromanische Säulengruppe
in der Benediktiner-Kirche von Offenbach am Glan

*Pillar-group, late Romanesque style,
in the Benedictine's Church at Offenbach on the Glan*

*Groupe de piliers de l'époque romane fleurie
dans l'église des Bénédictins d'Offenbach sur le Glan*

Schloß Guttenbrunnen (ehem. Louisenthal) bei Zweibrücken

Guttenbrunnen Castle (ancient Louisenthal) near Zweibrücken

Château de Guttenbrunnen (ancien Louisenthal) près de Zweibrücken

Herzogsvorstadt von Zweibrücken   *The Duke's suburb of Zweibrücken*   *Faubourg du Duc à Zweibrücken*

In einer Pirmasenser Schuhfabrik · Im Hintergrund die Stadt
In a factory of boots and shoes at Pirmasens, with the town in the background
Dans un atélier de cordonnerie à Pirmasens; la ville au fond

14

Stiftskirche von Kaiserslautern   *Cathedral of Kaiserslautern*   *Eglise collégiale de Kaiserslautern*

Kirchheimbolanden

urg Hohenecken
ei Kaiserslautern

Hohenecken Castle
ear Kaiserslautern

Château de Hohenecken
rès de Kaiserslautern

Der „Weinberg der Kirche" am Hauptportal der Klosterkirche Enkenbach
The "Vineyard of the Church" at the main porch of the conventual church of Enkenbach
La «vigne de l'église» au portail principal de l'église du couvent à Enkenbach

Spätromanische Säulengruppe der Klosterkirche von Otterberg
Late Romanesque pillar group of the conventual church at Otterberg
Groupe de piliers de l'époque romane fleurie dans l'église du couvent à Otterberg

Grabkammer Franz von Sickingens auf Burg Nanstein bei Landstuhl
Sepulchral vault of Franz von Sickingen at Nanstein Castle near Landstuhl
Sépulcre de Franz von Sickingen au château de Nanstein près de Landstuhl

Burgruine Altdahn in der Rheinpfalz
Castle ruins at Altdahn in the Palatinate
Les ruines du château-fort de Altdahn dans le Palatinat

22 Teufelstisch bei Hinterweidenthal   The "Devil's Table" at Hinterweidenthal   «Table du diable» près de Hinterweidenthal

Burg Drachenfels bei Busenberg   *Drachenfels Castle near Busenberg*   *Château de Drachenfels près de Busenberg*

23

Ausblick von den Dahner Burgen in den Wasgau
View from the castles of Dahn to the Vosges Mountains
Vue des châteaux de Dahn dans les Vosges

Im Wasgau · Links Burg Drachenfels
In the Vosges. Left side Drachenfels Castle
Les Vosges. A gauche le château de Drachenfels

Blick von Schloß Lindelbrunn   *View from Lindelbrunn Castle*   *Vue du château de Lindelbrunn*

Burg Berwartstein   *Berwartstein Castle*   *Le Château de Berwartstein*

Marktplatz von Annweiler
The market-square of Annweiler
Place du marché à Annweiler

Die Trifelsgruppe (im Vordergrund Annweiler)
The Trifels group, Annweiler in the foreground
La groupe du Trifels, avec Annweiler sur le devant

Friedhof und altes Rathaus von Dörrenbach
Im Detail: Renaissancestiege des Rathauses

Cemetery and old town-hall of Dörrenbach
In detail: Staircase of the town-hall, Renaissance-style

Cimetière et vieil hôtel de ville à Dörrenbach
Detail: Escalier de l'hôtel de ville (Renaissance)

Eindrucksvoller Renaissancebau in Bergzabern
(Gasthaus zum Engel)

Impressive Renaissance-building in Bergzabern
(Hostel "The Angel")

Bâtiment de la renaissance, plein d'effet, à Bergzabern
(Auberge l'Ange)

Gotischer Kreuzgang des ehemaligen Augustiner-Klosters von Landau
Gothic cross-vaulting of the ancient Augustine's monastery of Landau
Cloître en style gothique de l'ancien couvent des Augustins à Landau

Landauer Stiftskirche
der Grabkapelle

*edral of Landau
chapel of the grave

*édrale de Landau
chapelle du tombeau

In den Weinbergen der Pfalz · Im Hintergrund das Hambacher Schloß (Maxburg)
In the vineyards of the Palatinate. In the background the Castle of Hambach (Maxburg)
Dans les vignes du Palatinat. Au fond le château de Hambach (Maxburg)

34

Ausblick von der Madenburg in den Pfälzer Wald
View from Madenburg Castle to the Palatinate Mountains
Vue du château de Madenburg sur le montagne du Palatinat

35

In St. Martin   *In St. Martin*   *St. Martin*

Grablegung Christi in der katholischen Pfarrkirche von St. Martin (um 1520)
The sepulture of Christ in the Catholic Parish Church of St. Martin (abt. 1520)
Sépulture du Christ dans l'église parroquiale catholique de St. Martin (vers 1520)

Renaissancebau in Diedesfeld an der Weinstraße
Renaissance-building at Diedesfeld / Weinstrasse
Maison de l'époque Renaissance à Diedesfeld / Weinstrasse

Reizvolle Torbögen des ehemaligen Schlosses in Burrweiler
Attractive gate-arches of the ancient castle at Burrweiler
Attractifs cintres de porte de l'ancien château de Burrweiler

Marktplatz und Stiftskirche von Neustadt
Market-square and Collegiate Church of Neustadt
Place du Marché et Eglise du Couvent de Neustadt

In Edenkoben   *In Edenkoben*   *Edenkoben*

Ehemaliges Jesuitenkloster von Königsbach
Old Jesuites' monastery of Königsbach
Ancien monastère des Jésuites de Königsbach

In den Weinbergen um Gimmeldingen
In the vineyards around Gimmeldingen
Dans les vignes de Gimmeldingen

Sühnekreuz bei Deidesheim
The atonement-cross near Deidesheim
Croix de la Réconciliation près de Deidesheim

Im Kurgarten von Bad Dürkheim
In the park of the health-resort Bad Dürkheim
Jardin du quartier balnéaire de Bad Dürkheim

Sogenanntes Schlössel von Forst   *So called little castle of Forst*   *Le petit château de Forst*

Kallstadt
mit der
berühmten
Saumagen-
Weinstube

*Kallstadt
with the fame*
"hog's paunch
wine-room

*Kallstadt
avec la fameu*
taverne «Esto
de Porc»

Wachenh

Spätgotische Kanzel in Ruppertsberg
Late Gothic pulpit at Ruppertsberg
Chaire de l'époque gothique fleuri à Ruppertsberg

Altes Stadttor in Freinsheim
Old town-gate at Freinsheim
Vieille porte de ville à Freinsheim

51

Flachrelief am Eingang
des ehemaligen Marstalls
der Herren von Leiningen
in Grünstadt

*Flat relief at the entrance
of the old stables of the
noblemen of Leiningen
at Grünstadt*

*Demi-relief à l'entrée
de l'ancienne écurie
des Seigneurs de Leiningen
à Grünstadt*

Schmiedearbeit am Portal
des Augustinerchorherren-
stifts in Frankenthal

*Wrought iron-work
at the porch of St. Augustine's
Canons-Convent
at Frankenthal*

*Ouvrage en fer forgé
au portail du couvent
des chanoines d'Augustin
à Frankenthal*

52

Neuleiningen

Rathaus von Deidesheim   *The Town Hall at Deidesheim*   *La mairie de Deidesheim*

Im Hof der Hardenburg bei Bad Dürkheim
The court-yard of Hardenburg Castle near Bad Dürkhei
La cour du château de Hardenburg près de Bad Dürkhei

Apostelfigur
in der Pfarrkirche
von Neuleiningen

Apostle-statue
in the parish-church
of Neuleiningen

Statue d'un apôtre
dans l'église paroiss
de Neuleiningen

Barocker
St. Stanislaus Ko
in Laumersheim

Baroque statue of
St. Stanislaus Kos
at Laumersheim

Statue baroque
de St. Stanislas Ko
à Laumersheim

An den Ufern des Altrheins   *At the banks of the Old-Rhine*   *Aux bords du vieux Rhin*

Chor des Klosters Limburg an der Haardt   *Choir of Limburg Monastery on the Haardt*   *Chœur du couvent de Limburg / Haardt*

Im modernen Zentrum von Ludwigshafen   *Modern city center of Ludwigshafen*   *Centre ville moderne de Ludwigshafen*

Rheinhafen von Ludwigshafen   *The Rhine-port of Ludwigshafen*   *Port du Rhin à Ludwigshafen*

Das Altpörtel von Speyer   *The old gate-tower of Speyer*   *Vieille tour avec porte à Spire*

Speyer im Schatten des Doms *Speyer in the shadow of the Cathedral* *Spire, en l'ombre de la Cathédrale*

64   Der Kaiserdom in Speyer   *Speyer Cathedral*   *La cathédral des Empereurs à Spire*